AF585121

For Harvey, Adele & Ruby

Birds, Blooms & Bugs

Megan McKean

Hardie Grant
EXPLORE

Let's explore some backyards and gardens and see what we can find!

In the backyard, what do you see?
Birds perched on branches
in a big gum tree?

In the backyard, what can you spy?
Colourful flowers, or a beautiful
butterfly?

Can you find ...?
6 red roses
4 king parrots
3 garden gnomes

Out in the garden,
early and bright,
magpies warble in
the morning light.

In the veggie patch, what's
that popping through?
Tomatoes and strawberries
in red and pink hues.

Can you find ...?
3 magpies
2 basil plants
rake

Splashing in the pool,
what catches your eye?
Yellow-striped bees,
buzzing on by.

Can you find ...?

3 noisy
miners
beach
ball
2 water
dragons

Can you find ...?
3 galahs
4 jewel bugs
7 flying foxes

In the botanical gardens,
it's quiet and lush,
honeyeaters feast
on the red bottlebrush.

In the front yard,
where the wattles bloom bright,
a sleepy cat lounges,
basking in the sunlight.

Can you find ...?
6 yellow rosellas
gardening shoes
5 white daisies

Join our delicious picnic spread,
we have lots to share,
but watch out for the ants
scurrying everywhere!

Can you find ...?

watermelon slices

2 bottlebrush bushes

3 ibises

Can you find ...?
5 bees
2 skinks
3 watering cans

In the community
garden, shared by all,
sunflowers flourish,
standing proud and tall.

Can you find ...?
stick insect
2 azure kingfishers
3 cruiser butterflies

Down by the creek,
where the water flows,
dragonflies zip by
and a cool breeze blows.

On the balcony,
herbs and flowers grow,
brilliant bursts of colour,
potted in tidy rows.

Can you find ...?

pair of gloves

garden fork

2 cherrynose cicadas

Can you find ...?
thongs
2 sand crabs
8 silver gulls

Down at the beach,
what's that up in the sky?
Kites caught in the wind
and silver gulls flying high.

Sitting outside
at the corner cafe,
sparrows pick at your crumbs,
then swiftly flit away.

Can you find ...?
slice of cake
2 redback spiders
5 crested pigeons

Next to the footpath,
tiny gardens grow,
a snail slides along,
taking things nice and slow.

Can you find …?

letterbox

2 ringtail possums

2 crimson rosellas

In every backyard,
there's a colourful delight,
birds, blooms and bugs –
what a magical sight!

80 per cent of
Australia's plants
and animals can't
be found anywhere
else in the world.
Banksias are rich
in nectar; a perfect
snack for honeyeaters,
possums and bats.
Did you notice all of
these creatures in the
botanical gardens?
Australia is home
to more than 500
species of native
ladybirds.
Did you spot two
little ladybirds
hiding on every
page?
Golden wattle is the
Australian floral emblem –
bursting with the national
colours of green and gold.
Galahs mate for life.
True lovebirds!

The only egg-laying mammals both live in Australia – the echidna and the platypus.

Did you find one of each in this book?

While the crested pigeon has similar grey feathers to other types of pigeons, its black mohawk really sets it apart!

Butterflies taste with their feet! Their taste sensors are located in their feet, so they take in flavour by standing on their food.

Magpies are very social. They love wrestling and playing with other magpies, and even befriending humans.

Rainbow lorikeets are one of the most common birds in Australia, often flying together in big colourful flocks!

Did you find a rainbow lorikeet on every page?

Published in 2026 by Hardie Grant Explore, an imprint of Hardie Grant Publishing

Hardie Grant Explore (Melbourne)
Wurundjeri Country
Level 11, 36 Wellington Street
Collingwood, Victoria 3066

hardiegrant.com/explore

A catalogue record for this book is available from the National Library of Australia

Hardie Grant acknowledges the Traditional Owners of the Country on which we work, the Wurundjeri People of the Kulin Nation and the Gadigal People of the Eora Nation, and recognises their continuing connection to the land, waters and culture. We pay our respects to their Elders past and present.

For all relevant publications, Hardie Grant Explore commissions a First Nations consultant to review relevant content and provide feedback to ensure suitable language and information is included in the final book. Hardie Grant Explore also includes traditional place names and acknowledges Traditional Owners, where possible, in both the text and mapping for their publications.

Birds, Blooms & Bugs
ISBN 9781741179644

10 9 8 7 6 5 4 3 2 1

Publisher Tahlia Anderson
Project Editor Olivia Brown
Proofreader Siena O'Kelly
Design and Illustration Megan McKean
Typesetting Megan McKean
Head of Production Simone Wall

Colour reproduction by Splitting Image Colour Studio
Printed in China by LEO Paper Products LTD.

The paper this book is printed on is from FSC®-certified forests and other sources. FSC® promotes environmentally responsible, socially beneficial and economically viable management of the world's forests.